A *Leadingforward* REPORT

GROWING
YOUR OWN LEADERS:
Community Colleges Step Up

American Association of Community Colleges
with support from the W.K. Kellogg Foundation

Community College Press®
A Division of the American Association of Community Colleges
Washington, DC

The American Association of Community Colleges (AACC) is the primary advocacy organization for the nation's community colleges. The association represents more than 1,100 two-year, associate degree-granting institutions and more than 11 million students. AACC promotes community colleges through six strategic action areas: national and international recognition and advocacy, learning and accountability, leadership development, economic and workforce development, connectedness across AACC membership, and international and intercultural education. Information about AACC and community colleges may be found at www.aacc.nche.edu.

Author: Carol A. Jeandron
Editor: Donna Carey
Designer: Jennifer Gerstein, VC Graphics, Inc.
Printer: HBP Charter, Inc.

Printed in the United States of America
ISBN 0-87117-371-9

TABLE OF CONTENTS

PREFACE

In 2000, the American Association of Community Colleges (AACC) Board of Directors established a Leadership Task Force as part of a proactive effort to highlight leadership development in the association's mission. This focus has taken on greater urgency as states and institutions see an increasing number of retirements at every level, and the number of candidates qualified to fill those vacancies declines. Each year since 2001, more than 500 new, senior level administrators (e.g., chief academic, student services, or business officers) have been hired, and 80 to 100 new, first-time community college presidents have come onboard.[1]

The task force produced a statement, "Effective Community College Presidents," which identified essential leadership characteristics as well as effective components of leadership development programs. Following this lead, in summer 2003, with a grant from the W.K. Kellogg Foundation, AACC began an initiative known as Leading Forward.

Through Leading Forward, AACC launched a number of research, consensus-building, and planning activities, including four national leadership summits designed to address the challenges of developing leaders for community colleges. Summit participants included AACC member presidents; directors of university-based leadership programs; representatives from AACC Affiliate Councils; and representatives of single-campus, district, and state grow-your-own (GYO) leadership programs.

A key outcome of the Leading Forward planning activity was a set of core competencies (knowledge, skills, and values) for community college leaders based on input from the leadership summits. Community college presidents, summit participants, and AACC board members reviewed and refined the competencies. In April 2005, the AACC Board of Directors unanimously approved the document *Competencies for Community College Leaders*[2] and distributed it to community colleges nationwide. The work identified the following six core competencies as essential for community college leaders:

- Organizational strategy
- Resource management
- Communication
- Collaboration
- Community college advocacy
- Professionalism

---

[1]American Association of Community Colleges. (2006). Membership database (unpublished). Washington, DC: American Association of Community Colleges.

[2]American Association of Community Colleges. (2005). Competencies for Community College Leaders. Available from the Leading Forward Web site, www.ccleadership.org.

AACC developed an online leadership database that has grown steadily, demonstrating that institutions and individuals have identified specific needs and moved forward with a variety of strategies to fulfill those needs for their communities. Database entries include degree and non-degree programs at universities as well as programs within educationally based organizations such as the AACC Affiliate Councils.

In addition, many campuses, districts, and state systems have established GYO programs to identify potential leaders among current faculty, staff, and administrators and to groom them for advanced leadership positions. The GYO programs have emerged as a valuable and effective strategy. As the programs mature, some colleges have expanded their participation to include community members, allowing for increased interaction with individuals and organizations vital to the college.

The GYO programs provide positive examples of how community colleges go about solving challenges they face: by creating solutions in which they combine their own internal strengths with those available in their communities. This book documents how community colleges, districts, and states are taking charge in this critical area of developing leaders.

We are grateful to the W.K. Kellogg Foundation for its generous support of the Leading Forward initiative and this book. We extend appreciation to Courtney Larson, Nan Ottenritter, Cristina Blanco, Kathy Kirby, Margaret Rivera, Ellen Hause, and Lynn Barnett for their contributions to this project. Our thanks go especially to the presidents and program coordinators of the GYO programs across the country who shared their stories with us.

George R. Boggs
President and CEO
American Association of
Community Colleges

INTRODUCTION

In 2005, the American Association of Community Colleges (AACC) conducted a formal study of college, district, and state grow-your-own (GYO) leadership programs, which focus on developing future college leaders from among the existing ranks of midlevel administrators and faculty. This book reports the findings from that study and provides an overview of current institutional practices throughout the United States that might serve as helpful examples for other institutions seeking to build leadership programs. The book focuses on themes that recur among successful programs, especially in the areas of program characteristics, attendee characteristics, and outcomes.

AACC researchers developed survey questions from information gleaned from a study of Illinois community colleges, completed by the University of Illinois Office of Community College Research and Leadership, and from the work of AACC's Leading Forward initiative supported by the W.K. Kellogg Foundation. In addition, researchers conducted structured telephone interviews, contacted key program coordinators, and reviewed program materials such as application and evaluation forms. Unless stated otherwise, all quotations in this book came from interviews and written responses collected during the 2005 study.

Although a relatively small number of GYO programs currently exist, the researchers sought to create a diverse sample by considering geographic location; rural, urban, or suburban environment, and institutional size in the selection of colleges interviewed. The final sample included the following 16 community college programs, 2 community college district programs, and 5 state programs:

Community College Programs

Central Piedmont Community College (North Carolina)

Chemeketa Community College (Oregon)

Community College of Philadelphia (Pennsylvania)

County College of Morris (New Jersey)

Cumberland County College (New Jersey)

Frederick Community College (Maryland)

Metropolitan Community College (Nebraska)

Middlesex Community College (Massachusetts)

Midlands Technical College (South Carolina)

Mississippi Gulf Coast Community College (Mississippi)

Mount Wachusett Community College (Massachusetts)

Ocean County College (New Jersey)

Owens Community College (New Jersey)

Parkland College (Illinois)

Pitt Community College (North Carolina)

Southeastern Community College (North Carolina)

Community College District Programs

Academy for Collegiate Excellence, Collin County Community College District (Texas)

Consortium Leadership and Renewal Academy (CLARA), North Texas Community College Consortium (Texas)

State Programs

Asilomar Leadership Skills Seminar, Community College League of California

Chancellor's Leadership Seminar, Florida Community College System

Leadership Development Institute, Louisiana Community and Technical College System (LCTCS)

Community College Leadership Academy, Massachusetts Community Colleges

New Horizons Initiative, Kentucky Community and Technical College System (KCTCS)

AACC identified a contact person for each community college program and sent a preinterview questionnaire to facilitate the interview process. In most cases, that person had direct responsibility for planning and coordinating the activities related to the leadership development program, although at some colleges the contact person chaired a committee responsible for planning the initiative. In other cases, the contact person was the president or a staff member who worked with the president to plan and coordinate events.

Contacts had been at their institutions between 1 and 21 years; the median time was 2 years. More than two-thirds of the contact persons had not held positions at other community colleges. Their experience within the field of leadership development varied: Some had cofounded a state leadership program; some had worked within associations dedicated to leadership development; some had completed graduate work in community college leadership; and some had no prior experience within the field.

Results: At a Glance

The study revealed a number of recurring themes that serve as "how-to" recommendations for colleges seeking to build leadership programs:

Plan the Program

- Involve the president and ensure the support and commitment of the president, board of trustees, and all high-level administrators.

- Be inclusive in the planning stages. Outline roles and responsibilities. Appoint a person or designate a department to lead the effort who has the time and insight into the structuring, organization, and implementation of the program.

- Find funding sources that will help institutionalize the program.

Develop the Program

- Identify the audience. Select participants for their interest, enthusiasm, talent, and diversity.

- Provide a learning experience that adds to participants' knowledge about leadership and community colleges.

- Investigate a variety of models. Learn from other colleges and from promising practices in the field; however, make sure what you do fits your situation. "Don't adopt, adapt."

- Be flexible with the curriculum and modify as needed.

Deliver the Program

- Consider choosing presenters from among your own staff and resources.

- Include team building and networking as program features. Make some activities interactive.

Strengthen the Program

- Commit to program evaluation, including soliciting feedback from participants. Work for continuous improvement of the program.

- Recognize and celebrate success.

The following chapters elaborate on these findings with examples from the individual colleges, districts, and states interviewed.

1
WHY GROW YOUR OWN?

As in many fields, community colleges are seeing an increased rate of retirement among their leadership as the workforce ages. In response to the trend, colleges must find ways to increase the field of upcoming leaders. Grow-your-own (GYO) programs are one strategy. These programs are a recent trend among community colleges; of those studied, only one college GYO and one state GYO existed before 2000.

Several of the programs began as executive leadership programs, which stress campus-specific management techniques and provide general preparation for internal candidates to advance into mid-level or high-level positions at the institution. These programs differ from GYOs in that GYOs tend to take a more holistic approach, adding an emphasis on personal growth through the acquisition of leadership skills. These skills may help participants enhance their performance in their current and future positions in ways beyond just mastering standard management techniques.

The main reason respondents gave for starting leadership programs is demographics, including the challenge of replacing retirees. Metropolitan Community College (MCC) in Nebraska noted that 75% of the college population is older than 40. The college anticipates a 50% turnover in personnel by 2015. Thus, MCC considers its lead@mcc academy an investment in the future as the college provides its employees a structured opportunity to enhance their leadership skills through a program of self-assessment and skill development.

Leadership development programs may arise as part of a college's strategic planning process. Cumberland County College in New Jersey noted that its strategic plan includes three goals: literacy, learning, and leadership. In response to the third goal, the college initiated its Pathways Program: A Personal and Professional Development Program.

Community College of Philadelphia's Leadership Institute says its goal is "to establish a coordinated and sustained program of professional development for faculty and staff focused on mission achievement and educational effectiveness." The college encourages program participants to interact with leaders, understand self as a leader, gain broader perspective on issues, work collaboratively, and acquire specific leadership skills. Other community colleges, such as Owens Community College in New Jersey, initiated a leadership development program to facilitate a positive change in the college's culture, foster a spirit of collaboration, and enhance the concept of shared leadership.

Multicampus Mississippi Gulf Coast Community College (MGCCC) began its MGCCC Leadership Program to encourage a "one college" environment. According to the president, "the program allows participants to see that we are one college with similar issues and problems. [Participants] come to realize that we have more in common than we have differences." Many colleges expressed similar goals of enhancing interaction across divisions, departments, campuses, districts, and their states as a major impetus for starting leadership development programs.

Sometimes, the board of trustees encourages the college to begin a program. Board members of Frederick Community College in Maryland were directly responsible for initiating the executive leadership program and were active participants. Likewise, in statewide GYO programs, governing boards often urge colleges to start programs. The Louisiana Community and Technical College System (LCTCS) Board

of Supervisors recognized that the pipeline for future leaders was either nonexistent or disjointed and charged the LCTCS president with developing a program to address the future need for leaders. LCTCS president Walter Bumphus commented on the challenge and the responsibility:

> I liken [community college leadership] to a never-ending relay. We take positions as leaders and run as fast and as hard as we can, but we also need to understand and realize that at some point, we must pass the baton of leadership in a way that the other person in this relay will have a leg-up on the competition and be able to ultimately take the baton across the finish line.

The Kentucky Community and Technical College System (KCTCS) viewed the program as a way to build capacity through internal resources and to enhance its mission of building a learning organization focused on quality and service to students. Other governing boards saw state GYO programs as a cost-effective means to address concerns related to upcoming retirements and vacancies in senior-level positions.

As the state programs have developed, they have kept the focus on "growing" community college administrators by improving leadership and management abilities, upgrading skills, and broadening perspectives. For example, in 2001, the chancellor of the Florida Community College System created the Chancellor's Leadership Seminar, a professional development opportunity for midlevel managers seeking advancement to senior-level positions.

Statewide GYOs also emphasize reinforcing the organizational and leadership skills that employees can use in their current positions. The LCTCS Leadership Development Institute's stated objectives include the following:

> To develop employees that communicate more effectively, manage their time more efficiently, have a better understanding of others, have the ability to manage conflict, adapt and cope with change, build stronger teams, and raise awareness on ethics and values. These are characteristics that lead to successful leadership capabilities within one's current position or as he/she ascends within an organization.

The Asilomar Leadership Skills Seminar's stated purpose is to provide information, strategies, contacts, and

"I am convinced that today's 'leadership gap' creates more opportunities than it does challenges. For the numerous diverse women and men who aspire to leadership roles in our movement, the opportunities have never been better!"

opportunities for personal and professional growth. The program expects participants to acquire and successfully accept expanded leadership responsibilities within their own or other California community colleges.

Director Pamila Fisher noted: "I am convinced that today's 'leadership gap' creates more opportunities than it does challenges. For the numerous diverse women and men who aspire to leadership roles in our movement, the opportunities have never been better!"

2

PLAN THE
PROGRAM

The first step in developing a grow-your-own (GYO) program is to make sure the president and board of directors support the program. Presidents interviewed play various roles, from endorsing the program to organizing, funding, selecting participants, and conducting sessions. All the directors noted that the success of their GYO programs depends on presidential support and that this backing gives the program credibility on campus.

In North Carolina, Pitt Community College takes its mission to educate and empower people for success seriously. President Dennis Massey reported:

> The college's Leadership Institute is designed to help people realize their potential, even if at some point they decide to leave the institution. The Leadership Institute is one expression of my commitment to professional development and creating learning environments for employees.

Many respondents noted that buy-in and active involvement by the college president has been key to their success. One respondent reported that the president not only welcomes participants and

"The Leadership Institute is one expression of my commitment to professional development and creating learning environments for employees."

orchestrates a presidents' panel session but also conveys awards and generally makes participants feel valued. Program coordinators noted that presidents may perform various activities associated with the program, including approving curriculum and presenters, signing acceptance letters, teaching sessions, presenting awards, and giving the graduation address. One program coordinator summarized the president's involvement as "organizer, developer, speaker, and teacher."

Patricia Stanley, retired president of Frederick Community College, cited the importance of presidential support:

The Board of Trustees approved the executive leadership program as one of my annual goals, and I shared these goals with the college at convocation; [that is] the college community was aware that developing new leaders was a high priority. Without the support of the president's office, its importance to the college's future would have been greatly diminished.

Zelema Harris, president of Parkland College in Illinois, believes strongly in having the support of the board of trustees in leadership development initiatives:

The Board of Trustees and the president play a significant role in communicating the college's priorities to the entire college community. Leadership development must be an integral part of the strategic plan and the vision of the college. Board members by nature are concerned about the long-term viability of the college. Thus, succession planning is a major part of leadership development. Through Parkland's Leadership Development Program, new talent is identified, and professional development plans are implemented to support the goals of the participants and institutional needs. The board and president's commitment to the ongoing professional development of its employees communicates that they care about the value of each individual at the college; it communicates that promotions are encouraged within the college and that we are all learning to become a higher performing institution.

Choose a Home Base

Presidents must decide where to house the GYO program. Respondents mentioned various approaches, including housing the program in the office of the president, in the human resources office, among different divisions in a team approach, and within other offices.

Office of the President

Many colleges place the leadership development program in the office of the president. Examples include Frederick, Midlands Tech, Parkland, and Pitt. Brian Miller, assistant to the president and program coordinator at Pitt Community College, believes that housing the program in the president's office assures participants that the president has invested in the program and in them. Similarly, the leadership development program at Midlands Tech was immediately well received because of its presidential connection, which gave the program credibility and in turn allowed it to develop quickly.

Human Resources Office

At County College of Morris, the Employee Leadership Academy is housed in the human resources office. The director of human resources believes the entity that coordinates the program must have a broad institutional perspective and that the human resources office is appropriate because it is involved in planning for long-term succession. The office collaborates with all divisions, including academic affairs and business and finance, in planning the leadership program.

"The team brings together individuals of different temperaments, working styles, backgrounds, and areas of expertise."

Team Approach

At some colleges, a team rather than a single entity coordinates the leadership development program. At the Community College of Philadelphia, a team made up of the executive assistant to the vice president for academic affairs, the executive director of the library and learning resources, and a full-time faculty member coordinate the Leadership Institute (LI). Co-facilitator Joan Johnson finds the team approach advantageous:

> Working with a team of facilitators for the Leadership Institute has been an experience that parallels that of the participants in the LI. The team brings together individuals of different temperaments, working styles, backgrounds, and areas of expertise. We have learned in the past 4 years to play to our individual strengths. We also have a collective strength, knowing that we can rely on one another to get things done. We have learned to work together and to trust one another. We recognize our individual styles—particularly after 4 years of working with and through the Myers-Briggs Type Indicator—and embrace and respect them. We have seen the need for clearer goals and structure not only for the participants, but also for our team. The progress we have made in fine-tuning the LI and its associated activities has made us turn our thoughts to how we work. We operate differently and more efficiently and effectively than we did during the first LI.

Other Offices

Presidents also have chosen to assign responsibility for the leadership development programs to a wide range of other offices and personnel. In some institutions, for example, the programs are led by the director of admissions, vice president of student development services, vice president of administration, director of institutional advancement, or associate dean of resource development.

Set Program Parameters

Community colleges, districts, and state systems may have similar goals and intended outcomes for their leadership development programs, but program structures vary. Community college programs range from 18 to 63 hours. Participants may take part in program events for 3 to 14 days over 1 to 9 months. The shorter programs such as those at Parkland or Owens usually take place in a retreat setting and have an intensive schedule. The average leadership development program holds sessions 5 hours per day, 1 day per month, for 8 months. At the state level, half of GYO programs consist of yearlong events, and the other half offer an intense 3- or 4-day program. Most have a retreat component.

In the majority of leadership development programs studied, sessions are offered once a year, which coordinators note is sufficient to accomplish the goals and meet the needs of those interested in participating. Most are held while classes are in session, and most participants prefer Friday afternoons to avoid conflicting with faculty and staff schedules. The Midlands Technical College Leadership Development Program is typical, for example, in that eight of the nine sessions are held on Fridays between 1:00 p.m. and 4:30 p.m. during the fall semester.

The Management Institute of Ocean County College, which targets college supervisors while allowing other employees to participate, requires that all participants attend the beginning seminar "Management and Leadership: An Orientation to the Management Institute." Subsequent courses are arranged in a practical order to enhance skill development, and participants choose the courses they feel will benefit them. Two sections of each course are offered to accommodate schedules.

Programs vary not only in length but also in setting. The majority of colleges offer all sessions on campus. Some, however, offer the complete program in a retreat setting, and others use a combination of settings. Cost is often a factor in determining the setting.

Massachusetts Community College Leadership Academy's sessions are held on various campuses throughout the state to allow program participants exposure to various presidential leadership styles and to let them see firsthand what is happening at other colleges. The main host college plans the residency component, a 3-day culminating event whose goals are to provide fellows a variety of opportunities:

- In-depth exposure to community college leaders
- Opportunities for work on college projects and individual professional development
- Time to build networks for the future
- Opportunities to demonstrate communication skills

"It is important for the presidents to be closely involved with the fellows and expose them to opportunities on campus such as Executive Committee, Board of Higher Education, and Trustees meetings."

In addition, participants use retreat time to assess the initiative in order to provide feedback for organizers to use in planning future programs. Janice Motta, executive director of the Massachusetts Community College Presidents' Council, notes: "It is important for the presidents to be closely involved with the fellows and expose them to opportunities on campus such as Executive Committee, Board of Higher Education, and Trustees meetings."

The Florida Chancellor's Leadership Seminar is an intensive 3-day workshop held in June in a hotel. The KCTCS program consists of a fall seminar held in a hotel with a follow-up retreat in the spring, held off site at the system office.

Organizers of the women's Asilomar Leadership Skills Seminar credit part of the program's success to its setting at the Asilomar State Conference Grounds in Monterey Bay. The goals of the program include reflection and networking, which are more easily realized in this natural, unique environment.

Identify Funding

GYO leaders take different approaches to funding their programs, which range in cost from $2,200 to $75,000 annually. Coordinators suggest that the per-person cost ranges from $25 to $3,000. At none of the colleges studied did participants have to pay to take part. The majority of colleges indicated funding for GYO programs is derived from the professional development line of the college's operating budget. Other sources of funding include the president's budget, foundation grants, state funding, human resources or academic affairs budgets, and the general operating fund. The funds, whatever their origin, generally cover items such as presenter honoraria, meals and receptions, participant books and other materials, and graduation events. In some cases, the funds cover transportation and lodging expenses.

One community college allocates $50,000 from its human resources budget for customized workshops and seminars on campus and $25,000 for conferences and seminars off campus. This amount includes fees, related expenses for independent contractors, printing, supplies, and expenses associated with off-campus events. Another college allocates $10,000 in human resources funding for the GYO program. At other colleges, funding for the leadership development programs comes from the academic affairs budget. One institution has a separate line item of $7,000 for GYO events.

Colleges are creative. One reported it uses the president's discretionary funds to purchase refreshments; another allocates $45,000 from the special projects line in the president's budget for GYO expenses. At one college interviewed, the office of planning and development allocates approximately $172 per participant; at another, the Center for Leadership and Staff Development funds the program at a

---

Funding Sources for Grow-Your-Own Programs

Community College Programs

Internal Budgeting	External Budgeting
Professional Development	Foundation grant
President	State funding
Human Resources	
Academic Affairs	
General Operating	
Center for Leadership and Staff Development	
Office of Planning and Development	

State and District Programs

Host college
Systems office
Sponsor

rate of $25 to $30 per attendee. Some colleges allocate foundation grants or state money to professional development through leadership programs; one college taking this approach is considering charging a minimal fee to departments who sponsor participants.

Typical Program Expenses

Printed materials (handouts and books)

Lodging

Transportation

Speaker's gifts or honoraria

Meals and refreshments

Kick-off luncheon and graduation event

Colleges that hold GYO activities off campus tend to have larger budgets than those that hold all activities on campus; those with the larger budgets may allocate funding for expenses related to transportation, lodging, and meals. One college allocates $20,000 from the operations budget to hold a 3-day retreat for 20 participants; another allocates $20,000 from an institutional and staff development budget to provide lodging and meals for approximately 60 participants in the 2-day retreat portion of the program.

Funding for many state GYO programs comes primarily from the participants' colleges. In one state, participants can apply for scholarships if college funding is not available to support them. In another program, participants or their sponsoring colleges pay the cost of travel, hotel accommodations, some meals, and a $50 registration fee. Sponsors may provide additional funding.

The Louisiana and Kentucky programs are funded at the system level. The budgets fluctuate each year depending on the number of participants and the number of speakers. Funding and support for these programs has proven strong and flexible. For example, during the 2005 Hurricane Katrina and Hurricane Rita catastrophes, the Louisiana Community and Technical College System covered all of the expenses for its program, easing the financial burden for the colleges and demonstrating a commitment to leadership development.

3
DEVELOP THE PROGRAM

Publicize

Colleges advertise and promote their leadership development programs differently, but common approaches include word of mouth (which many think is the most effective), e-mail, and Web notices. A letter from the president on Parkland College's Web site invites college personnel to apply for the Leadership Development Seminar. Interested persons must submit an application, which contains the caveat that those selected are expected to attend all sessions. Community College of Philadelphia's Web site includes information on past and current Leadership Institutes, as well as an application form, details of each session, and past group projects. Frederick Community College invites potential applicants to a luncheon to learn more about the program. (*For a sample invitation letter, see Appendix A*).

Colleges spread the word through announcements at events such as convocations, faculty senates, college council and departmental meetings, and presentations by past participants. Program coordinators also use customary printed materials such as brochures, flyers, newsletters, and notices in local newspapers to advertise events.

Pitt Community College provides a Web site, information packets, invitations from the president, and testimonials from past participants describing the benefits of the program. In addition, personal communications encourage individuals not accepted to the previous Leadership Institute to submit their application again.

Identify Eligible Participants

The community colleges, districts, and states studied full-time faculty and administrators accepted into the leadership development programs; in most cases, full-time staff also were eligible to apply. A few colleges allow part-time faculty to participate. Generally, colleges require participants to have 1 or 2 years of tenure.

State programs do not seem to have a length of service requirement, although individual college presidents may require this in selecting employees to participate. The Louisiana Community and Technical College System (LCTCS) stipulates that participants must be employees in mid-level positions or faculty members who have at least 60% release time for administrative duties (defined as directors, deans, assistant deans, or others in comparable positions). Collin County Community College District requires that applicants for its Academy for Collegiate Excellence (ACE) be full-time faculty or professional staff, hold a minimum of a master's degree, and have worked a minimum of 3 years in higher education.

Enrollment in the California program is open to those in any leadership position, including classified managers, trustees, and leaders of senates and unions. Florida seeks midlevel managers who possess proven leadership capabilities, as indicated through previous leadership experiences and accomplishments such as supervisory, management, budgeting, policy, advising, public relations, and advocacy. All Kentucky Community and Technical College System (KCTCS) faculty and staff are eligible to apply.

Application Process

The application process varies among colleges, ranging from no formal application to a rather lengthy one. At some colleges, in addition to the expected resumes and letters of commitment for full participation, programs require fairly thorough descriptions of experience (professional and volunteer), career goals, letters of reference, and what applicants expect to gain from the leadership program. Other examples of application criteria include the following:

- Answers to specific questions about leadership: Community College of Philadelphia asks what leader the applicant most admires; asks the applicant to describe a personal leadership experience, how he or she was effective or ineffective in that situation, and what the applicant learned from it; and asks what the applicant can contribute to the Leadership Institute.

- Documentation of college and community activities: The selection committee at County College of Morris seeks individuals that through their actions (college and/or community) have demonstrated an interest in being contributing members.

- Supervisory support: Southeastern Community College requires written confirmation that a supervisor will support the applicant's attendance at all activities related to the Institute for Today's Leaders. Owens Community College requires a formal agreement between the applicant and supervisor. Collin County Community College District requires a confidential letter from immediate supervisors.

- Interview: At Metropolitan Community College and Owens Community College, applicants must meet for an interview with a committee or review panel.

Mount Wachusett Community College's program has no formal application process for entrance into its Leadership Academy. It is open to all employees, and everyone who expresses interest is allowed into the program.

Among the state programs in general, the application process mirrors the college processes: application forms signed by the college president, resumes, and letter(s) of recommendation. Collin County Community College District also requires a statement of long-term goals and a current job description. (*For a sample application form, see Appendix B*).

Selection Process

Just as the application process varies among colleges, so does the selection methodology, although most use some kind of review committee. At the majority of colleges, a committee selects the final participants, or a committee reviews the applications and the president, vice president, or program director make the final selections. Membership on these selection committees varies. Metropolitan Community College's selection committee is composed of a human resources employee and executive employees. Each member receives a packet of applications and completes a selection form. The selection committee meets, deliberates, and chooses the participants.

The committee for the Leadership Institute of Central Piedmont Community College in North Carolina includes a representative from each college unit. At County College of Morris, the selection committee includes deans and directors, but the President's Cabinet grants final approval of the selectees.

At Chemeketa Community College in Oregon, the Leadership Development Team that plans the LifeLong Leaders program also selects the participants. The team includes a planning and development specialist, the director of emergency services and physical education, human resources personnel, a faculty member, an Upward Bound employee, and an employee in disability services.

Pitt Community College's 2006 selection committee team consists of the president; faculty from arts and sciences, construction and industrial technology, and business; and staff from accounting and the president's office. Midlands Technical College's Executive Council selects participants based on commitment to leadership, professional experience, and reason for applying to the program.

Some colleges do not use a selection committee at all. At the Leadership Management Institute of Middlesex Community College in Massachusetts, the program's coordinator and the vice president of academic and student affairs select participants. At Frederick Community College, interested employees apply directly to the president, who selects participants. At Parkland College, the president and vice president select participants.

For statewide programs, in most cases college presidents have the primary responsibility for selecting participants from eligible and interested personnel on their campuses. For the North Texas Consortium Leadership and Renewal Academy (CLARA), college presidents set criteria, screen applicants, and sign application forms. Each of the 28 member institutions may nominate as many people as it wants to; however, if the total number is too large, each president may be limited to selecting two. The consortium president then approves and signs the application.

The LCTCS Leadership Development Institute allows each college to develop an internal process for selecting one nominee from the college. The institute also has six at-large spots for individuals to apply directly to the system. A system-level screening committee selects participants for the at-large slots based on completion of the leadership development institute application, which includes letters of recommendation and a personal statement. The selection committee seeks applicants who have exhibited initiative and demonstrated that they are emerging leaders.

The California program selects applicants on a first-come, first-served basis. In Kentucky, the KCTCS president makes the final selection of participants, incorporating gender and minority equity as well as faculty-to-staff ratio in the process. In Texas, the Collin County Community College District program co-directors review application packets and, based on selection criteria, make recommendations to the president and the leadership team for final approval.

GYO programs may use other approaches. For example, for the Cumberland County College Pathways Program, the selection committee draws names of 15 applicants per year from bins representing different staffing categories. The college encourages those who are not randomly selected to apply the next year. (*For a sample selection criteria form, see Appendix C*).

Diversity

Approximately 50% of the community colleges indicated they target specific groups among which are supervisors, faculty, midlevel managers, and staff assistants. A majority of the colleges indicated a deliberate effort to include a diverse representation of people in terms of gender, ethnicity, race, age, years of employment, and current positions at the college.

Community College of Philadelphia emphasizes diversity in gender, minority status, and role, as evidenced by the demographics the program has maintained in its 4 years of existence. Judith Gay, vice president for academic affairs, described the strategy and its effect:

> From the application process to the forming of project teams, we are intentional about mixing styles, backgrounds of experience, and organizational positions. It is human nature to gravitate toward others who are 'like' you, so our selection process with attention to diverse college representation and the use of the Myers Briggs to determine type is important in creating a diverse experience in the group's work as a whole and in the project teams. One participant commented that if she had not been assigned to a team, she definitely wouldn't have had such a rich experience in which she learned not only about other people's jobs but also how different approaches to a problem could enlighten her own thinking.

Chemeketa LifeLong Leaders program's selection criteria note that organizers are "seeking a broad cross-section of Chemeketa staff and faculty with diversity

"From the application process to the forming of project teams, we are intentional about mixing styles, backgrounds of experience, and organizational positions."

in work roles, length of time at the college, gender, cultural background, etc."

State and district programs also emphasize diversity among participants; the LCTCS program, for example, indicates on the application that the participants selected will be diverse in gender and ethnicity. Jesse Jones, President, North Texas Community College Consortium, noted the advantages: "Participants come from many different positions in business affairs, student affairs, and academic affairs. This wide representation in each group has made for rich and broad perspectives and networking."

Hal Higdon, vice president of administration and coordinator of the leadership development program at Mississippi Gulf Coast Community College, stated:

> We try to achieve diversity in our [Leadership Program] classes, not just administration, staff, and faculty, but also by gender and race. This is important to ensure that the process is deemed fair by all employees and because it is important that you are working to ensure a diverse group of future leaders.

Develop the Curriculum

GYO programs choose and develop curriculum in various ways. Chemeketa Community College conducts college-wide surveys or needs assessments requesting input on the topics from potential participants. The program coordinators supplemented this information by conducting an extensive research of literature and other college leadership development programs. Ocean County College develops its curriculum through a continual needs identification process resulting in additional courses offered throughout the year. Mississippi Gulf Coast Community College researches existing GYO programs and adapts appropriate ones to fit the college's needs.

Metropolitan Community College's GYO curriculum is developed by the participants themselves at the initial 2-day retreat, during which participants explore what leadership is and then relate it to the self-assessment questionnaire they completed before the retreat. Using a consensus process, the participants identify areas for skill and knowledge development they want to pursue over the 9-month period of the program. They then develop the curriculum using all of this feedback.

In other cases the president, a planning committee, an external consultant, or human resources makes the decisions regarding program curriculum. The Central Piedmont Community College GYO program developed curriculum in conjunction with the human resources department, whose personnel brought expertise in "hard" skills such as interviewing processes and budget management. The director of the Center for Leadership and Staff Development was responsible for the "soft" skills such as communication and managing time and emotions, and the president oversaw the entire curriculum development process. At Frederick Community College and Parkland College the presidents were primarily responsible for deciding program curriculum.

How curriculum is developed also varies among the statewide and district GYOs. At KCTCS, the system president and a national consultant choose the curriculum. In some cases current participants play a role in determining program curriculum. Some examples include the following:

- The 2004–2005 Texas CLARA participants prioritized major themes and issues such as finding and developing an appropriate leadership and management style; the modern community college; personnel assessment and evaluation issues; effective communications; dealing with change; using technology to enhance administration and teaching-learning; building professional resources and networks, and budget and finance.

- Massachusetts designed its curriculum based on evaluations and input from the previous participants and a survey of current fellows. Recent topics included community college history and mission; leadership theories, concepts, practices; understanding complex academic public organizations; community college students and diversity; resource development and management; assessment and accountability.

- The California GYO program includes key topics not readily available elsewhere but critical to survival and success. These topics include campus politics; understanding and working with constituencies; building coalitions; working with trustees; and an in-depth exploration of issues related to diversity and inclusiveness. One content session focuses on community college finance and budget strategies.

- The Louisiana program initially developed curriculum in response to the system's needs for specific leadership characteristics. As the program evolved, coordinators changed the curriculum to reflect system-identified needs and to include broader leadership issues. Nationally recognized figures serve as presenters for session topics such as report on national perspectives of leadership; the making of a leader; conflict management; legal issues in higher education; understanding the role of economic and workforce development in community and technical colleges; the role of technology in the pursuit of providing cutting edge programs and services for students; institutional effectiveness: the importance of research in decision making; and the art of fundraising, grant development, and management. (*See also the sidebar "Suggested Topics for Program Sessions"*).

Most of the GYOs studied based their curriculum on specific leadership competencies that may be grouped under the six competencies identified in AACC's *Competencies for Community College Leaders*. Respondents rated the competencies as either "very" or "extremely" essential to the effective performance of a college

Suggested Program Topics

- The Makings of a Leader
- Can You Really Have it All? Achieving a Healthy Balance Between Personal and Professional Life
- Ethics in Leadership
- Civility and Diversity
- Legal Issues in Higher Education: Facing Leadership Challenges
- Conflict Management
- Leading From the Middle: The Importance of Customer Service to Employees and Students
- Effective Hiring Practices
- How to Hire and Manage Good People
- Management Versus Leadership: Moving From Peer to Supervisory/ Management Strategies

- Project Management
- Understanding the Role of Economic and Workforce Development in the Community and Technical College
- Engaging the Community in the Community College
- Institutional Effectiveness: The Importance of Research in Decision Making
- A Leader and His/Her Constituents: Reaching Out to a Variety of External Stakeholders
- Bringing in the Money and the Students: Promoting Your Institution
- The Art of Fundraising, Grant Development, and Management
- Budgeting

leader. Following are descriptions of the competencies along with a summary of how programs might consider each competency in planning the program curriculum:

- **Organizational strategy: An effective community college leader strategically improves the quality of the institution, protects the long-term health of the organization, promotes the success of all students, and sustains the community college mission, based on knowledge of the organization, its environment, and future trends.**

Program participants explore the concept of organizational strategy through several topics, such as collective leadership, strategic planning and goal setting, legislative affairs, community expectations, and economic development.

- **Resource management: An effective college leader equitably and ethically sustains people, processes, and information as well as physical and financial assets to fulfill the mission, vision, and goals of the community college.**

Topics covered under this competency include finance and governance, interviewing and hiring, budgeting, and grant writing.

- **Communication:** An effective community college leader uses clear listening, speaking, and writing skills to engage in honest, open dialogue at all levels of the college and its surrounding community, to promote the success of all students, and to sustain the community college mission.

  Program planners include several topics related to being an effective communicator. These include advanced communication skills, constructive confrontation, communication styles, and journal writing.

- **Collaboration:** An effective community college leader develops and maintains responsive, cooperative, mutually beneficial, and ethical internal and external relationships that nurture diversity, promote the success of all students, and sustain the community college mission.

  Participants acquire knowledge of this competency through team-building activities and information on organizational cultural diversity, high performance coaching and mentoring, and partnership building.

- **Community college advocacy:** An effective community college leader understands, commits to, and advocates the mission, vision, and goals of the community college.

  Topics covered under this competency include building a learner-centered college, understanding the history and purpose of two-year colleges, learning how to be a college ambassador, and studying trends in college teaching and learning.

- **Professionalism:** An effective community college leader works ethically to set high standards for self and others, continuously improve self and surroundings, demonstrate accountability to and for the institution, and ensure the long-term viability of the college and community.

  Participants are exposed to information dealing with professionalism, including lifelong learning, responsibility in the workplace, motivation, recognition, and leadership excellence.

4
DELIVER THE PROGRAM

Deliver the Content

Leadership development programs use a variety of methods to deliver content. All programs use face-to-face meetings. Central Piedmont Community College, Community College of Philadelphia, Middlesex Community College, and Parkland College also have an online component to their programs. The Massachusetts grow-your-own (GYO) program uses the online Blackboard management system to communicate among fellows and the instructional team. Several programs have plans to incorporate an online strategy in upcoming leadership programs.

The most frequently employed teaching methods include mentoring and job shadowing, individual or group projects and presentations, readings and papers, and lectures. Some colleges also use attendance at leadership or community college-related meetings and discussion boards.

Mentoring and Job Shadowing

Fifty percent of the colleges incorporate an experiential component, and several of the others plan to add it in the future. The most common experiential methodology involves one-on-one strategies such as mentoring and coaching. Southeastern Community College incorporates a mentoring component as part of a 10-hour internship required of program participants.

Frederick Community College wants to expose potential leaders to different leadership styles, so each participant has a mentor. Mentors guide participants through a project outside their usual work areas, which helps them learn about the mentor's area and leadership style.

Mississippi Gulf Coast Community College initiated mentoring and job shadowing in the third year of its GYO program. Participants and mentors must come from different departments and different campuses of the multicampus college. Job shadowing allows participants to spend the day with people who have

Mentoring

Participant Benefits

- Exposure to different leadership styles

- Exposure to different departments or campuses

- Guidance with individual and group projects

- Feedback on written assignments

- Discussion of leadership issues, including challenges

Who Mentors

- Program instructional team member

- Leader on participant's campus

- Leader on another campus

- Current supervisor

already achieved positions to which they aspire. In some cases, the experience may help participants realize that these jobs are not what they want after all and that they prefer to stay in their current position.

Metropolitan Community College incorporates mentoring by involving supervisors of participants in both small and large group interaction throughout the program. Once selected, participants and their immediate supervisors meet with the program coordinator. At this meeting the participant and supervisor sign a learning agreement and set up expectations together. They then receive a link to an online assessment to complete

on their own by a specific deadline. After the assessment is completed, they meet to interpret results of the assessment. At the initial 2-day program retreat, participants reach consensus about topics to be covered and discuss different leadership styles with their assessment used as the basis of the discussion. Metropolitan Community College considers its mentoring strategy to be an important part of its leadership development program.

All statewide and district programs incorporate a mentoring process. The California program has an informal mentoring program. The Consortium Leadership and Renewal Academy (CLARA) program requires its participants to have a mentor in connection with the required individual projects.

The Massachusetts program requires each fellow to be assigned an instructional team member who serves as a mentor to a group of 6 to 7 fellows. Each participant submits written assignments and holds discussions on projects and other issues with the mentor. Also, during the 3 days of the residency component of the program, members of the instructional team meet with fellows in coaching sessions to discuss professional development accomplishments, challenges, and next steps.

Participants in the Louisiana program select their mentors based on their own goals. Mentors must have system approval before the relationships commence. Mentors provide support for the participants throughout the program as it relates to their leadership plans and short-term goal attainment.

Projects

The majority of colleges reported using team-based or individual projects, papers, and presentations. For example, for County College of Morris's midsession project, small groups select a nonprofit organization to visit and then report back to the class. Southeastern Community College's Institute for Today's Leaders incorporates small group interactive activities to enhance networking and team building. All participants take the Myers Briggs Type Indicator inventory; program leaders make team assignments based on the results to ensure diversity in work groups. This arrangement provides opportunities for participants to work on projects with people who have different traits and work styles.

Community College of Philadelphia's team projects are an important component of its Leadership Institute. The project development process takes place during the fall semester when the team identifies a problem or challenge, submits preliminary summaries, conducts research, consults colleagues outside the leadership program, works with a mentor, and submits a proposal. During the spring semester, the team presents the proposal to the college community, may apply for a mini grant to support the project, develops prototype, completes research, implements the project, and presents final reports at the ending session of the Leadership Institute. Past team projects include: "A New Student Guide to Starting Classes at Community College of Philadelphia," "Men of Color–Path to Power," and an alumni speaker series.

Mary Griffin, co-facilitator of the Community College of Philadelphia's Leadership Institute, reports that project team assignments are an important component of the learning experience:

> We use employee categories and job titles to ensure that members of different groups (faculty, administrative, and classified or confidential), representing different areas of the college, work together. We also make racial, ethnic, and gender diversity a priority within each team. Finally, each team includes members with a diversity of skills, strengths, experience, and areas of expertise. Our ongoing assessment clearly indicates that interaction within teams enhances participants' self-awareness and appreciation of difference.

Ocean County College holds a team building regatta. Through the challenge of sailboat racing, participants learn essential tools for building positive, constructive work teams. Setting a course and sailing a boat require developing a strategy, understanding and tapping crewmembers' unique strengths and talents, and above all communicating clearly with all the crew. Facilitators lead a workshop after the regatta to discuss the skills participants brought, the roles they played, and how this team behavior relates to the roles participants play at the college.

> "Our ongoing assessment clearly indicates that interaction within teams enhances participants' self-awareness and appreciation of difference."

Massachusetts' statewide GYO program incorporates two projects, the College Project and the Leadership Reflection Project. The College Project, planned in consultation with the president, provides an opportunity for fellows to demonstrate their leadership within their college community and to develop a product that responds to specific needs and interests of their college. The Leadership Reflection Project provides an opportunity for fellows to reflect on leadership in general and on their own leadership in particular. It also encourages fellows to identify areas for professional growth and development and to pursue these in a supportive, coaching atmosphere.

Sample Group Projects

Pilot Program: Academic Transition for Students on Academic Probation
Develop a plan to increase the retention of students at the college by working collaboratively with the academic departments and their students who have been placed on academic probation. Ensure that academic policies are fair and apply to all students.

Guide to Community College Enrollment
Create a flow chart of the step-by-step process to enrollment.

Why Are So Many Textbooks Unavailable for Students at the Start of the Semester?
Identify the reasons, causes, and effect on student engagement and persistence.

Improving Communications: Enhancing Quality Customer Service Through Professional Development Training
Create a plan to help employees better understand what quality customer service is, increase morale, and demonstrate positive customer service behaviors in daily performance.

Men of Color: Path to Power
Identify ways the college can increase retention of incoming African American and Hispanic males (e.g., through a series of seminars on academic and social issues of interest to the group.)

Focus on Core Values: An Awareness and Implementation Campaign of the Student Code of Conduct
Develop ways to raise campus awareness of issues related to academic integrity in general and the Student Code of Conduct in particular.

Map to Success
Design a foldout map to show students where to go for help on a number of critical issues that contribute to academic persistence and success.

CLARA's individual project requirement has resulted in many worthwhile endeavors including the following products: Excellence in Advising Students–A Resource Guide; Improving the Hiring Process; Redesign of the Cedar Valley College Web Site: Phase I; Fire Academy and Fire Technology Course Needs Survey and Assessment Study for Program Validation and New Program Development; and Comprehensive Financial Reporting System for Grayson County College.

Collin County Community College District divided participants into two groups. One group played a major role in the administrative retreat and led an all-college strategic planning program. The second group focused on improving communication across the district. Members conducted a study of current communication practices and made recommendations of ways to improve communication at the multicampus district.

Networking is seen as a valuable aspect of group projects. California team projects are completed on site. They include creating skits and songs that provide many networking opportunities. An applicant from the CLARA program notes, "Networking is a key to being a successful leader, and through CLARA I will have the opportunity to expand my resources." (*See also the sidebar "Sample Projects"*).

Readings and Papers

The majority of community colleges incorporate readings into their GYO programs. Central Piedmont provides program participants a notebook with articles, syllabi, assessments, and a reading list. Ocean County College requires some readings in advance of the program and also recommends follow-up readings. Participants at Community College of Philadelphia, Middlesex, and Owens incorporate required readings into group discussions, reaction papers, and personal reflections. At other colleges, session facilitators recommend certain readings, but none are required.

Similar patterns follow in state and district GYO programs. The Massachusetts GYO program requires fellows to select and review literature and best practices on the subject of their project and to complete readings prior to each seminar. CLARA and Louisiana also use readings for focused discussions. The Asilomar Leadership Skills Seminar does not incorporate a required reading list, but speakers recommend specific articles and books connected to their topics. Collin County Community College District provides participants copies of articles and a list of recommended texts from which to select and write reaction papers.

Identify Speakers

All colleges reported that personnel from their institution present lectures or teach some or all of the leadership development sessions. Programs also use personnel and presidents from other community colleges, personnel from system offices, and other consultants. Less frequently, programs enlist nationally known figures and personnel from universities. Those colleges with more funding tend to use the national resources more frequently than do colleges with limited funding.

Central Piedmont Community College encourages community colleges to look at their internal resources, to "trade" with other nearby colleges, and to collaborate whenever they can. Middlesex Community College identified personnel who had completed leadership development programs elsewhere or who were in doctoral leadership programs and used them as resources. Lexy Sanchez-Riffe, program coordinator at Chemeketa Community College, reminds program planners to "look under rocks to find some of those folks on campus that aren't just the 'usual suspects.'"

Community College of Philadelphia uses external as well as internal presenters. Internal personnel present sessions on budget and finance, institutional research, leading change, grant writing, decision making, identifying leadership styles, and building effective teams. External consultants may present sessions on local, state, and national environmental scans; conflict management; diversity; and leadership and emotional intelligence.

Most statewide and district programs use experienced leaders of member institutions and employees with specific expertise at the system office as session presenters. Some also invite national and, in some cases, international leaders to address the participants on specific topics. The program agenda often includes panels or presentations by current or past community college presidents, as with the Chancellor's Leadership Seminar in Florida. The presidents as well as board commissioners play a major role in presenting sessions, including Traits of an Educational Leader, Challenges of Leadership, Strategic Planning, Advancing to the Top: Personal and Professional Challenges, Case Studies on Ethics, and Case Studies and Current Issues in Leadership.

5 STRENGTHEN THE PROGRAM

Evaluate

Most colleges report having participants evaluate their experience at the end of each session as well as after the conclusion of the program. Cumberland County College has participants evaluate each day of the program and may choose to incorporate changes immediately. The college evaluates its program regularly to enhance the program's "interest and relevance" for participants. Community College of Philadelphia evaluates after each session, at midpoint, and at the end of each program. The planning group uses data to organize the next year's program. Presenters receive feedback as well.

The Mississippi Gulf Coast Community College leadership team, session presenters, and program participants are all part of the evaluation process. Mount Wachusett Community College uses the program Survey Monkey to develop

and distribute an online evaluation for each session and at the end of the program.

Metropolitan Community College acquires written feedback from participants at the end of each session and at the end of the program. In addition, the program coordinator meets with past participants in a focus group, clarifies the feedback offered in the evaluations, and discusses the program's strengths and areas for improvement. The planning group uses this information to modify its next program. Collin County Community College District's evaluation process also includes input from a focus group.

Central Piedmont Community College began by asking participants to evaluate three times—at the end of each part; the evaluation process includes feedback given to the presenter at the end of each session and discussion led by the college president. In the future, the evaluation process will include supervisors of participants assessing changes that can be attributed to participation in the program.

As with the community college grow-your-own (GYO) programs, statewide and district leadership development programs recognize evaluation as a key component to continuous improvement. The Consortium Leadership and Renewal Academy (CLARA) evaluates each session as well as the entire program. The Kentucky, California, and Louisiana GYO programs also use evaluation forms to gather participant feedback that helps improve the programs. (*For sample evaluation forms, see Appendix D and Appendix E*).

Program Completion Data

In addition to using formal evaluations, several colleges track program completers to determine the program's effectiveness. Because many of the programs are relatively new, some of the tracking systems are still in the planning stage. The majority of programs that currently track completers use informal methods, including word of mouth and human resources providing information about promotions. Central Piedmont Community College, Metropolitan Community College, and Southeastern Community College are among the small number of colleges that have a more formal method involving a tracking database.

Colleges measure program success using several factors, some tangible and some less tangible. The most common criterion is promotion of participants. At Community College of Philadelphia, more than one-third of participants have moved up the career ladder. At Midlands Technical College, 10% of its full-time employees have completed the program. Several have received promotions, for example, interim department chair, faculty council chair, staff council chair elect. Other colleges, including Central Piedmont, Metropolitan, Middlesex, Parkland, and Southeastern, also have recorded upward mobility among participants. Although the programs cannot guarantee the participants would not have advanced anyway, respondents expressed the opinion that the GYO programs have had a positive influence on participants' career mobility.

Although the majority of participants, including those promoted, remain at their colleges, some have moved into higher-level positions at other colleges. Zelema Harris, President, Parkland College, summarized the perspective of many presidents:

> Parkland's program is geared for the development of our own faculty, staff, and administrators; however, we recognized from the beginning of the program that some leaders may find opportunities outside Parkland. Fortunately, those participants who wanted to stay at Parkland and assume traditional leadership positions have been able to do so. Others find that the leadership experience has helped them to expand their role within their own positions. Some have stated that they are no longer bound by the job description and can assist the college in many ways, by serving on committees, teams, and by enhancing their knowledge to serve students better. Those few who have left we hope have fond memories of the experiences they had at Parkland. And, we need supporters within the college as well as outside the college.

"Others find that the leadership experience has helped them to expand their role within their own positions. Some have stated that they are no longer bound by the job description and can assist the college in many ways, by serving on committees, teams, and by enhancing their knowledge to serve students better. Those few who have left we hope have fond memories of the experiences they had at Parkland. And, we need supporters within the college as well as outside the college."

In addition to promotions, tangible outcomes include projects or creative products, such as artwork, promotional products, or a strategic plan. A team of Cumberland Community College participants created a decorative sculpture using their interpretation of the key words of the college's mission, vision, and values. Another team created a promotional CD and involved students in the production. The CD cost approximately $12,000, compared with an estimated $50,000 to have a promotional CD produced by a public relations firm. Ocean County College's program participants took on the rewriting of culture statements as a project. As a result of projects undertaken by participants of Frederick Community College's program, the college now has a teaching and learning center, an international and global initiative, and an alumni association.

To measure success, programs also consider increased participation in college initiatives, enhanced participant skills, and participants' enrollment in advanced degree programs. During a collegewide professional development program at Community College of Philadelphia, Leadership Institute participants facilitated 17 of the 20 roundtable discussions. The college also noted that participants enhanced their skills in areas such as grant writing and communication. Mississippi Gulf Coast Community College reported that several participants entered doctoral programs.

Coordinators of the leadership development programs at all of the colleges studied also reported less tangible outcomes. The majority saw an increase in collaboration across disciplines, networking, teamwork, self-confidence, community involvement, committee participation, and communication.

Colleges noted that after completing the program, participants had less of a "faculty versus staff" attitude, greater awareness of personality types and respect for others, enhanced listening skills, and a better understanding of how their unit or area fits in to the college. Midlands Technical College and Mississippi Gulf Community College, both multicampus colleges, found that their programs had the effect of building valuable networks among colleagues that bridged the campuses together. In addition, supervisors reported that participants' effectiveness in current positions had improved and they had become more involved in community activities.

Statewide program participants also reported tangible outcomes. The Kentucky Community and Technical

College System (KCTCS) Teaching and Learning Support Services unit at the system office tracks completers by name, college, year of participation, faculty or staff classification, gender, race, employment title or status when selected, and employment title or status to present date. Through this tracking system, KCTCS confirmed that 24 of the participants have been promoted within their college or to the system office. The Asilomar Leadership Skills Seminar reported that at least two dozen program alumni have become community college presidents, and the majority of participants have received promotions.

In addition to promotions, participants report receiving acknowledgment awards, continuing education credit, or certificates. In some cases, attendees receive credit at a degree-granting institution. Massachusetts fellows may request that participation in the academy be treated as a graduate-level course (4 credits) and may enroll for credit in the Education Policy, Research and Administration Department of the School of Education at the University of Massachusetts–Amherst. CLARA participants can receive graduate credit in the Higher Education program at the University of North Texas.

As with the community college programs, the state leadership programs notice tangible outcomes of participation in projects. The Florida Chancellor's Leadership Seminar notifies potential candidates during the application process that they must be willing to identify and commit to working on a leadership project for the sponsoring college. Among the projects completed by participants are a new student advisement system, integration of the registration process on a branch campus into the entire campus, and a computerized system for ordering textbooks for the college bookstore.

System heads and college presidents also reported that participants in general have exhibited an increased level of self-confidence and willingness to take on leadership roles. They show increased participation on committees and projects, reflecting an eagerness to improve the college and promote the system.

A participant in the leadership program of the Collin County Community College District summed up the experience with the Academy for Collegiate Excellence (ACE):

> As an ACE fellow, participants gain a wealth of information that will enhance leadership performance, sharpen skills with critical knowledge from understanding operational aspects, cost centers, and budgets to identifying various employee work styles, setting performance goals, and executing a strategic plan. [Participants] learn the role of the president and board relations, how to multitask and complete assignments, how to confidently set expectations for self and others, and how to understand current legal and public policy issues facing higher education.

Modify the Program

At most colleges the content, methodologies, or program delivery methods have changed over the years, usually as a result of evaluation and other feedback from participants.

Community College of Philadelphia has observed positive effects by moving from individual projects to group projects with a given theme. Central Piedmont Community College has added more components and participant interaction to its program. Middlesex Community College has moved from an emphasis on senior managers talking about their road to leadership to more case studies and interaction. The program also has added a mentoring component. Overall, changes across programs include a shift from lecture to more interactive methods; addition of more external speakers, online components, and mentoring; and a move from individual to group projects.

Reward and Celebrate Success

Participants in the GYO programs studied nearly always receive some type of tangible reward as a sign of successfully participating and completing the program. Most typical is a plaque or certificate, but rewards may include college or continuing education credit. Mount Wachusett Community College participants receive 3 hours of credit that appears on Mount Wachusett's transcripts for the course Perspectives in Leadership. Participants have been able to transfer the credit into university programs. Participants at Ocean County College and Owens Community College also may be awarded credit at a degree-granting institution.

At Ocean County College, participants receive certificates after completion of each workshop. Those who complete six courses receive a Management Institute certificate and special recognition.

Mississippi Gulf Coast Community College acknowledges graduates with special program shirts—a different color for each year.

Most of the colleges have graduation or commencement events to celebrate the participants' successful completion of the GYO program. County College of Morris lists commencement as the last item on the agenda of its Employee Leadership Academy programs. Community College of Philadelphia holds a College Honors Tea to present certificates and awards to Leadership Institute participants, who are also featured on the program's Web site. Southeastern Community College holds a graduation attended by the board of trustees and the participants' supervisors; the college president gives the graduation address.

At Metropolitan Community College's celebration ceremony, executive staff and supervisors attend as participants and informally step up and share what the experience has done for them. Kay Friesen, director of professional development and coordinator of the GYO program, noted, "Before, [participants] would not have been comfortable enough to stand up in front of their supervisors and share their growth, strengths, and weaknesses. Their stories show how much they have learned and how they did not want things to end."

Celebrating is also a common practice in state and district GYO programs. The Kentucky program has two points of celebration. After the fall segment, participants attend a luncheon, which provides an occasion for them to express their thoughts on the program. At the end of the spring retreat, coordinators hold an official ceremony and distribute certificates to participants. The Massachusetts Community College Leadership Academy closes its Residency College with an awards ceremony. The Division of Community Colleges and Workforce Development in Florida hosts a Chancellor's Leadership Seminar Reunion Reception for participants of all classes that have completed the program.

Success stories abound. The program coordinator at Chemeketa Community College, related one such story:

> A student had been at the college for about 8 years holding various positions. Between juggling work and family, she had difficulty taking classes to complete her degree. When she first heard about LifeLong Leaders, she was intrigued but had concerns about being accepted and felt intimidated by the idea of attending classes with directors, faculty, and others. With some prodding from her supervisor, she applied and was accepted. She was pretty quiet for the first few meetings, shared information only when asked, and rarely mingled with other attendees. By the end of the year she was actively participating and even leading group work. In response to what had brought about the change in her, she shared her initial concerns about not feeling "smart" and "capable" around the other participants. She did not think she had anything to share or teach them; however, she came to realize that everyone was there to learn from one another and that in this program the "playing field" was equal. The LifeLong Leaders program was a setting where people could leave their titles/positions at the door. She now

participates on several collegewide committees and has facilitated a session for the current LifeLong Leaders cohort.

A graduate of Pitt told his own story:

> I had been at Pitt Community College for almost 15 years and had moved into a position administering job training. While in this position I decided that I wanted more from my career, and the Leadership Institute helped me to see how I could accomplish this goal. Since completing the program, I have been promoted to coordinator of the Weekend College program here at PCC. The Leadership Institute helped me to build the strong foundation that I need to be successful in this position. The institute also allowed me to spend time with other PCC employees who have similar interests and career goals. I was able to meet both formally and informally with old friends and new colleagues to share ideas. This helped to create stronger, more trusting relationships within our PCC team. Overall I feel that the Pitt Community College Leadership Institute experience was very valuable to me. It helped me to learn how to grow as a leader and encouraged me to help others strive for their goals as well.

> "Since completing the program, I have been promoted to coordinator of the Weekend College program here at PCC. The Leadership Institute helped me to build the strong foundation that I need to be successful in this position."

"Participants overwhelmingly report greater confidence in themselves to take leadership positions, and indeed 42 percent of our first two graduating classes have been promoted to positions of greater responsibility. Given the right environment to learn about and exercise leadership skills and demonstrating genuine belief that the leader inside can emerge, people do rise to expectations."

Susan Tobia, Leadership Institute Co-Facilitator, Community College of Philadelphia, summarized the success of her program:

> As facilitators, we feel very proud of our graduates as we observe the leadership roles they increasingly take in the institution. Participants who may not have been previously noticed as leaders have eagerly accepted requests to serve on committees and collegewide initiatives, to lead cross-unit discussion groups, and to take on greater responsibilities in their departments and in their communities. As one participant said, 'I know now I can be a leader.' The Leadership Institute is seen as a prestigious program, and the opportunity to interact with local and national leaders reinforces the powerful broadening experience that engenders increased confidence in skills of communication, problem-solving and decision-making, important skills that our future leaders will need in addressing the mission of community colleges with their diverse needs. Participants overwhelmingly report greater confidence in themselves to take leadership positions, and indeed 42% of our first two graduating classes have been promoted to positions of greater responsibility. Given the right environment to learn about and exercise leadership skills and demonstrating genuine belief that the leader inside can emerge, people do rise to expectations.

CONCLUSION

This publication includes many stories, but it highlights one outstanding theme among the interview responses: The benefits of grow-your-own (GYO) programs far outweigh the dollars invested. Some benefits are personal—achieving a promotion, feeling empowered to make the next career move, or no longer feeling bound by a job description. In addition, some benefits clearly help the college as a whole, as participants seek to make greater contributions by joining special committees, or they find ways to use their newfound knowledge to better serve their students. Colleges gave examples of tangible benefits they received when program graduates brainstormed and created a new student advisement system, integrated a registration process on a branch campus into the entire campus, and created a computerized system for ordering textbooks for the college bookstore.

The majority of colleges studied reported that they saw an increase in collaboration across disciplines, networking, teamwork, self-confidence, community involvement, committee participation, and communication. States found that expanded programs that included participation from all the community colleges in the system helped increase participants' understanding of the state system as a whole.

What began as relatively simple programs to grow leaders for college campuses have turned into programs that have had many additional bonuses that influence colleges and communities. GYO programs provide an impressive example of how community colleges can confront a problem head-on, identify a simple yet ingenious solution, and then share their solutions with other colleges. Through GYO programs, the colleges continue to create a climate of learning and leadership for their communities.

ABC Community College Leadership Institute
Sample Invitation To Apply

March 3, 2007

Dear Colleague:

The ABC Community College Leadership Institute seeks to promote "home-grown" leaders from within the ABC community. In recognition of your experience with and commitment to the college, we invite you to apply to share in this unique professional development opportunity.

The institute is limited to 25 participants and will feature individual professional development and team-building activities. The college will provide lodging, meals, and conference materials.

The goals of the ABC Community College Leadership Institute are as follows:

- Identify and develop individual leadership competencies
- Promote interaction and networking across college divisions
- Build problem-solving skills
- Analyze ABC in the context of state and national models

The institute will include a series of professional talks and interactive sessions presented by local and state leaders in higher education. Program topics will include the following:

- Community College History and Mission
- Leadership Skills for Community College Employees
- Using Critical Success Factors as a Leadership Tool
- Building Professional Resources, Networks, Budget and Finance
- Being an Effective Communicator

The institute is a working session that will require preparation and follow-through (case studies, individual professional development plans); however, we hope you will find it an opportunity to join in some fun with your ABC colleagues as well.

If you are interested, please complete and return the enclosed application to John Smith, ABC Development Coordinator, by March 25, 2007. ABC College offers this program annually to expand the leadership potential among our employees and to promote teamwork across the institution. Although we cannot accommodate all applicants every year, we encourage you to apply as we endeavor to make the program available to as many eligible applicants as possible.

If you have any questions or suggestions as we coordinate the ABC Community College Leadership Institute, please contact John Smith at 555-555-1212.

Sincerely,

Jane Jones
ABC Community College President

ABC Community College Leadership Institute
Sample Application

I. Personal Information

Name of applicant:_____

Title:_____

Campus/office location: _____Campus extension:_____

Supervisor: _____

II. Employment History

Date of hire at ABC Community College:_____/ _____/ _____
$\qquad\qquad\qquad\qquad$ (mo/day/yr)

Please indicate your most recent employer prior to ABCCC:

Name of institution/organization: _____City/State:_____

Title:_____

Primary responsibilities: _____

_____

Dates of employment: From _____/ _____/ _____/   to _____/ _____/ _____
$\qquad\qquad\qquad\qquad$ (mo/day/yr) $\qquad\qquad\qquad\qquad\qquad\qquad\qquad$ (mo/day/yr)

III. Education

List colleges/universities attended, degrees received, and specialized training.

Name of College/University (City, State)	Dates (from–to)	Degree Earned

IV. Application and Attachments

The following items must be submitted for consideration:

☐ Completed application

☐ Letter of interest, including a statement of your long-range professional goals

☐ Resume

☐ Current job description

☐ Confidential letter of endorsement from your immediate supervisor

☐ Request for supervisor support form

Submit the application, letter of interest (your reasons for applying to the ABC Leadership Institute), resume, and current job description in one envelope to ABC Leadership Institute Coordinator, John Smith. The confidential letter of endorsement and the request for supervisor support form must be sent directly to Jane Jones, community college president, by your immediate supervisor.

I understand that if I am accepted as a participant in the ABC Leadership Institute I am expected to attend and participate in all sessions and will use my acquired knowledge and leadership skills to enhance the future of ABC Community College.

Applicant's Signature: _____ Date: _____

I will fully support participation in this activity if this employee is selected to the ABC Leadership Institute.

Supervisor's Signature: _____ Date: _____

ABC Community College Leadership Institute
Sample Selection Criteria Form

Applicant Name: _____

1. Employment Category (Check appropriate category)

Faculty _____FT _____PT

Administrator _____FT _____PT

Classified/Confidential Employee _____FT _____PT

2. Commitment   (Please check all that apply)

Candidate's Signature   _____

Department Chair or Immediate Supervisor's Signature   _____

Please assign quality points for #3–#6 below based on the following scale:

Missing	Inadequate	Adequate	Exceptional
0	1	2	3

3. Indication of Service   Fill in points in space provided

To the college   _____

To the community   _____

As a leader (either college or community)   _____

4. Philosophy of Leadership

Identifies leader   _____

Links qualities of leadership to leader   _____

45

5. Self-Awareness as Leader/Potential Leader

Identifies professional situation where leadership
was called for   _____

Reflects on effectiveness/ineffectiveness of leadership
strategies in that situation   _____

Explains lessons learned   _____

Links reflection on situation to philosophy of leadership (#4) _____

6. Potential Contributions to Leadership Institute

Articulates ways of contributing to institute   _____

First positive reference   _____

Second positive reference   _____

Total number of points   _____

ABC Community College Leadership Institute
Sample Self-Evaluation Form

Use the scale below to reflect your self-evaluation. Feel free to add a short comment beneath your rating or to add comments at the end of the evaluation form.

1	2	3	4	5
Strongly Agree	Agree	Don't Know	Disagree	Strongly Disagree

_____1. I have interacted with and gained insight from leaders in various fields related to the mission of the community college.
Comments to myself:

_____2. I have an increased awareness of the local, state, national, and global contexts within which the college will function in the 21st century.
Comments to myself:

_____3. I have an increased understanding of specific ways in which the larger environment may affect the college in the pursuit of its mission.
Comments to myself:

_____4. I have developed an increased self-awareness as a leader and an understanding of my leadership style.
Comments to myself:

_____ 5. I have a better understanding of the organizational structure and organizational culture of the institution.
Comments to myself:

_____6. I have increased my knowledge of resource allocation, budgeting, and finance.
Comments to myself:

_____7. I feel that I am part of a collaborative network of problem solvers.
Comments to myself:

_____8. I have had the opportunity to work collaboratively on a project of interest to me and of benefit to the college community.
Comments to myself:

_____9. I gained insights from my mentor that will be helpful to me.
Comments to myself:

_____10. I have gained a deeper understanding of the college mission, vision, and values.
Comments to myself:

ABC Community College Leadership Institute
Sample Program Evaluation Form

Please write a short paragraph in response to each of the following questions.

1. What insight(s) related to the mission of the community college did you gain from leaders you met through the program?

2. One of the goals of the program was to increase your understanding of specific ways the local, state, national, and global environment may affect community colleges. Give an example of your increased understanding in any of these contexts.

3. How has your understanding of the organizational culture of the college changed, if at all?

4. How have you applied your knowledge of resource allocation, budgeting, and finance in your work?

5. How, if at all, have you made use of the connections you formed with colleagues since participating in the program?

6 What did you learn from your participation in the team project?

7. How have you applied what you have learned in the program in your work?

8. Have your career goals changed? If so, how?

9. What would you change for future participants?

10. Please identify, by number, any session(s) that should be deleted or changed next time. If they should be changed, how?

11. a. What are your expectations for leadership activities following this seminar?
    b. What type of follow-up sessions would be helpful to support these expectations?

12. What specific information would you like to know as you continue to explore leadership at ABC?

Thank you for taking the time to complete this evaluation.
Your comments will help us strengthen the program.

Program Contacts

This appendix contains a complete list of campus, district, and state community college grow-your-own (GYO) programs contacted by AACC for the GYO Leaders study. All contact names listed were current as of the date of publication.

Community College Programs

Central Piedmont Community College
PO Box 35009
Charlotte, NC 28235
Program Name: CPCC Leadership Institute
Contact: Diann P. Back
Title: Director, The Center for Leadership and Staff Development
Ph: 704.330.4392
Email: diann.back@cpcc.edu
www.cpcc.edu

Chemeketa Community College
4000 Lancaster Drive NE
Salem, OR 97309
Program Name: Life Long Leaders
Contact: Lexy Sanchez-Riffe
Title: Planning and Development Specialist
Ph: 503.399.6995
Email: lsanch14@chemeketa.edu
www.chemeketa.edu

Community College of Philadelphia
1700 Spring Garden Street
Philadelphia, PA 19130
Program Name: Leadership Institute
Contact: Susan Tobia
Title: Executive Assistant to the Vice President for Academic Affairs
Ph: 215.751.8356
Email: stobia@ccp.edu
www.ccp.edu/vpacaff/leadership_institute/

County College of Morris
214 Center Grove Road
Randolph, NJ 07869
Program Name: County College of Morris Employee Leadership Academy
Contact: Rob Stoto
Title: Director, Human Resources
Ph: 973.328.5039
Email: rstoto@ccm.edu
www.ccm.edu

Cumberland County College
PO Box 1500, College Drive
Vineland, NJ 08362-1500
Program Name: Pathways Program: A Personal and Professional Development Journey
Contact: Catherine Mack
Title: Assistant to the President, Special Projects
Ph: 856.691.8600
Email: cmack@cccnj.edu
www.cccnj.edu

Frederick Community College
7932 Opossumtown Pike
Frederick, MD 21702
Program Name: Executive Leadership Program
Contact: Carol W. Eaton
Title: President
Ph: 301.846.2442
Email: ceaton@frederick.edu
www.frederick.edu

Metropolitan Community College
PO Box 3777
Omaha, NE 68103-0777
Program Name: lead@mcc Academy
Contact: Kay Friesen
Title: Director of Professional
    Development and Events
Ph: 402.457.2878
Email: KFriesen@mccneb.edu
www.mccneb.edu

Middlesex Community College
591 Springs Road
Bedford, MA 01730
Program Name: The Leadership
    Management Institute
Contact: MaryAnne Dean
Title: Dean, Professional and Resource
    Development
Ph: 781.280.3580
Email: deanm@middlesex.mass.edu
www.middlesex.mass.edu

Midlands Technical College
PO Box 2408
Columbia, SC 29202
Program Name: Midlands Technical
    College Leadership Development
    Program
Contact: Kelly Tribble
Title: Curriculum Coordinator
Ph: 803.822.3426
Email: tribblek@midlandstech.edu
www.midlandstech.edu

**Mississippi Gulf Coast Community
    College**
PO Box 609
Perkinson, MS 39573
Program Name: MGCCC Leadership
    Program
Contact: Hal Higdon

Title: Vice President for Administration
Ph: 601.928.6234
Email: hal.higdon@mgccc.edu
www.mgccc.edu

Mount Wachusett Community College
444 Green Street
Gardner, MA 01440-1000
Program Name: Mount Wachusett
Community College Leadership Academy
Contact: Diane Greb
Title: Assistant Vice President, Human
    Resources & Affirmative Action
    Officer
Ph: 978.630.9160
Email: D_Greb@mwcc.mass.edu
www.mwcc.edu

Ocean County College
College Drive, PO Box 2001
Toms River, NJ 08754-2001
Program Name: Ocean County College
    Management Institute
Contact: Deborah Robinson
Title: Director, Business Education &
    Training
Ph: 732.255.0509
Email: drobinson@ocean.edu
www.ocean.edu

Owens Community College
PO Box 10,000
Toledo, OH 43699
Program Name: Owens Leadership
    Academy
Contact: Gretchen Carroll
Title: Director, Owens Leadership
    Academy
Ph: 567.661.7234
Email: Gretchen_carroll@owens.edu
www.owens.edu

Parkland College
2400 West Bradley Avenue
Champaign, IL 61821
Program Name: Leadership: A
    Commitment to Involvement in the
    Decision-Making Process at Parkland
    College
Contact: Tom Ramage
Title: Vice President, Academic Services
Ph: 217.351.2542
Email: ramage@parkland.edu
www.parkland.edu

Pitt Community College
PO Drawer 7007
Greenville, NC 27835-7007
Program Name: Pitt Community College
    Leadership Institute
Contact: Brian Miller
Title: Assistant to the President
Ph: 252.493.7421
Email: bmiller@email.pittcc.edu
www.pittcc.edu

Southeastern Community College
PO Box 151
Whiteville, NC 28472
Program Name: Institute for Todays'
    Leaders
Contact: Julie Stocks
Title: Vice President, Student
    Development Services
Ph: 910.642.7141
Email: jstocks@sccnc.edu
www.sccnc.edu

State and Community College District Programs

Collin County Community College District
2800 East Spring Creek Parkway
Plano, TX 75074
Program Name: Academy for Collegiate
    Excellence
Contact: Juanita Austin
Title: Dean, Development Education
Ph: 972.881.5721
Email: jaustin@ccccd.edu
www.ccccd.edu

Community College League of California
2017 O Street
Sacramento, CA 95814
Program Name: Asilomar Leadership
    Skills Seminar
Contact: Pamila Fisher
Title: Leadership Consultant, Chancellor
    Emeritus, Yosemite Community
    College District
Ph: 916.444.8641
Email: pamfisher@gorge.net
www.ccleague.org

Florida Community College System
Turlington Building, Suite 1514
325 West Gaines Street
Tallahassee, FL 32399
Program Name: Chancellor's Leadership
    Seminar
Contact: J. David Armstrong
Title: Chancellor, Community College
    and Workforce Education
Ph: 850.245.9449
Email: david.armstrong@fldoe.org
www.fldoe.org

Kentucky Community & Technical College System
300 North Main Street
Versailles, KY 40383
Program Name: New Horizons Initiative
Contact: Jan Muto
Title: Assistant to the Chancellor for Teaching and Learning
Ph: 859.256.3328
Email: jan.muto@kctcs.edu
www.kctcs.edu

Louisiana Community and Technical College System
265 South Foster Drive
Baton Rouge, LA 70806
Program Name: LCTCS Leadership
Development Institute
Contact: Angel M. Royal
Title: Executive Assistant to the President and Vice President for External Affairs
Ph: 225.922.2815
Email: aroyal@lctcs.net
www.lctcs.net/ldi.html

Massachusetts Community College
Old South Building
294 Washington Street, Suite 301
Boston, MA 02108
Program Name: Massachusetts
Community College Leadership Academy
Contact: Jan Motta
Title: Executive Director
Ph: 617.542.2011
Email: jmotta@mcceo.mass.edu
www.massccla.org

North Texas Community College Consortium
PO Box 310800
University of North Texas
Denton, TX 76203-1337
Program Name: Consortium Leadership and Renewal Academy (CLARA)
Contact: Jesse Jones
Title: President
Ph: 940.565.4035
Email: jjones@unt.edu
www.unt.edu/ntccc/WkspConf/CLARA_Program_Description.htm

REFERENCES

American Association of Community Colleges. (2006). Membership database (unpublished). Washington, DC: American Association of Community Colleges.

American Association of Community Colleges. (2005). Competencies for Community College Leaders. Available from the Leading Forward Web site, www.ccleadership.org.